SWASTICK BOOK BOX
MASON OF WINNERS

SBB

Cursive WRITING BOOK Capital Letters

Awesome Cursive Writing Practice Book for Kids

By: **Preeti Garg**

Follow the patterns with your pencil.

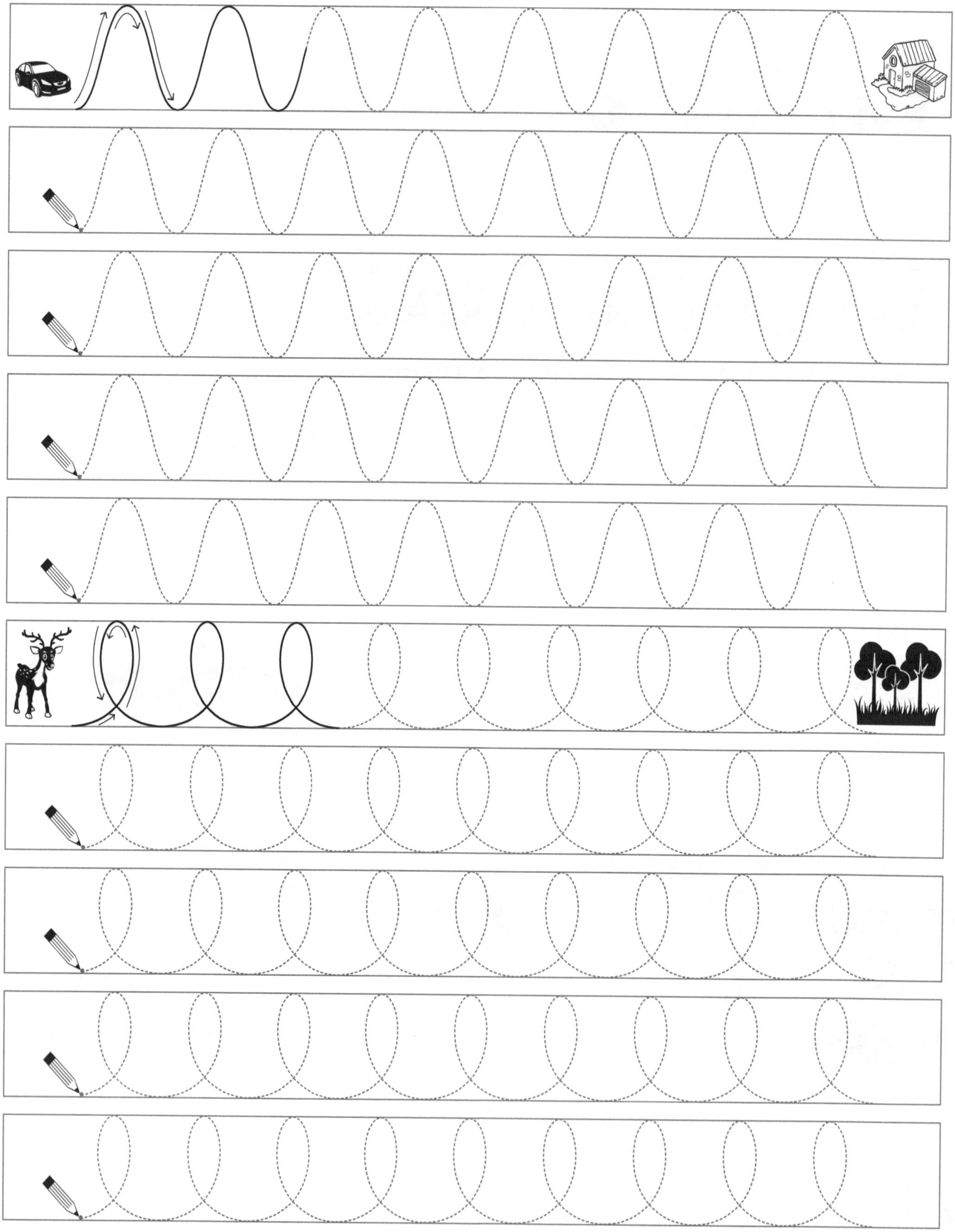

Follow the patterns with your pencil.

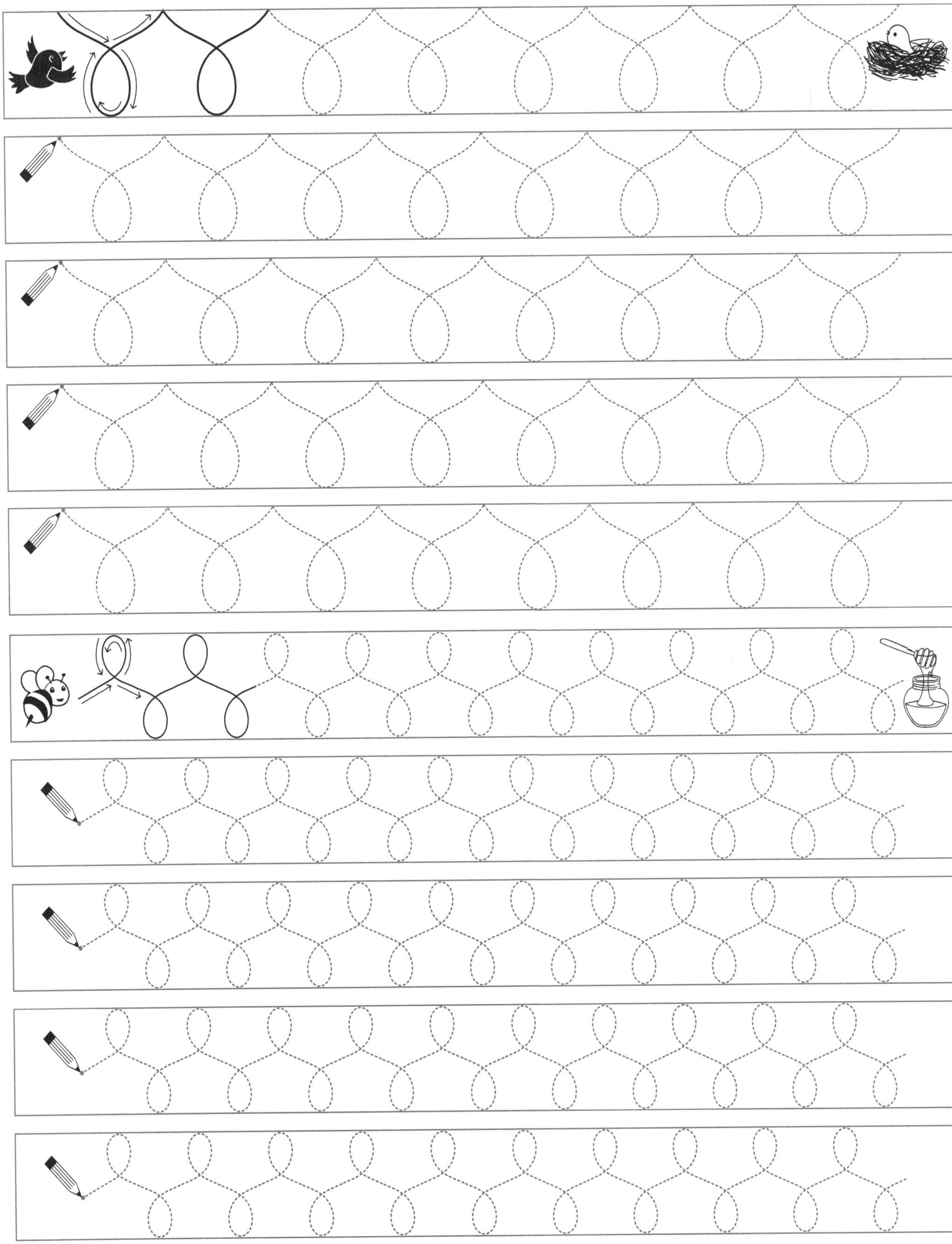

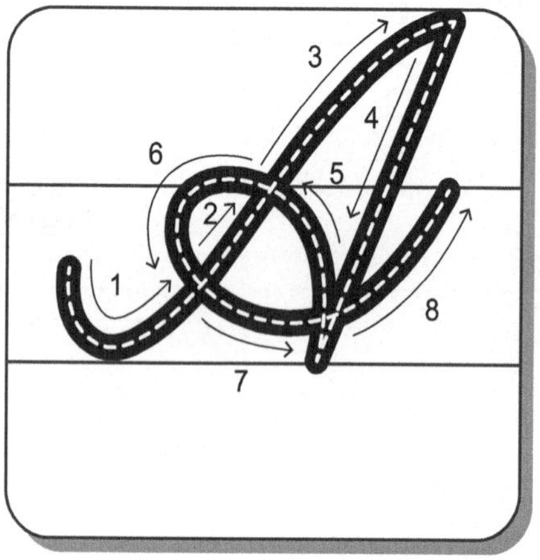

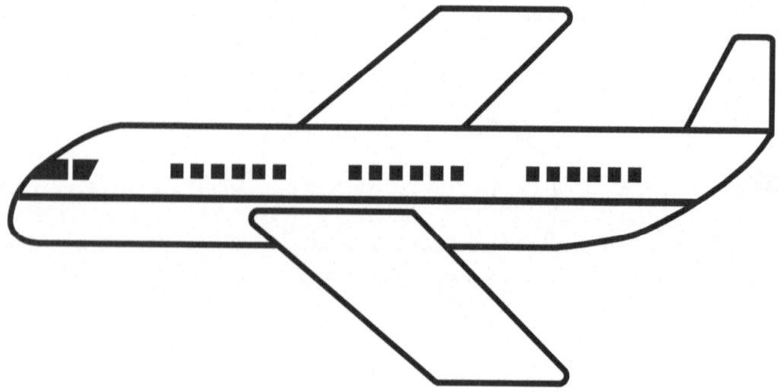

Aeroplane

Date : ....

Teacher's Signature : ....

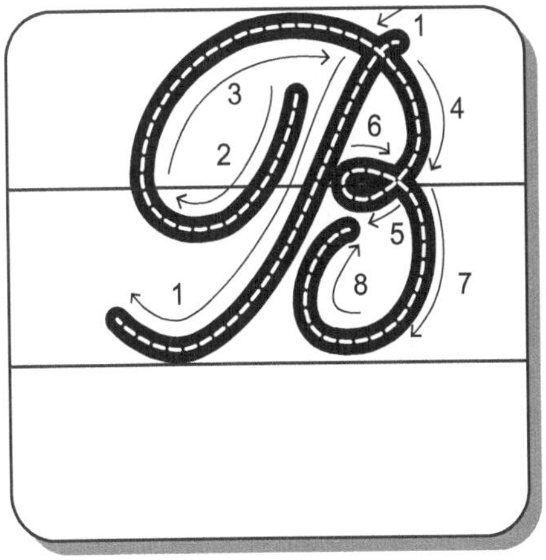

Butterfly

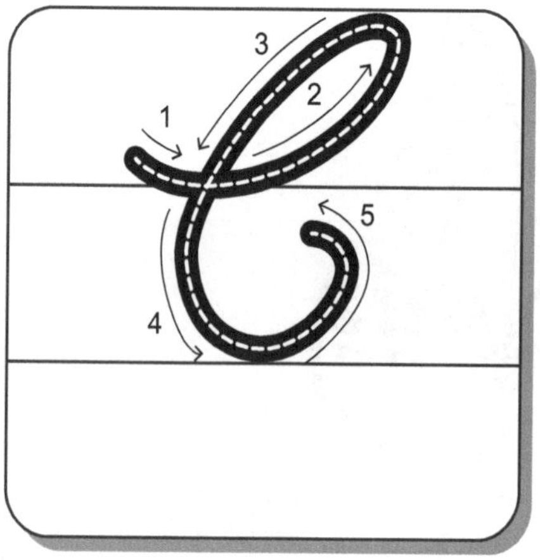

Cap

Date : ....

Teacher's Signature : ....

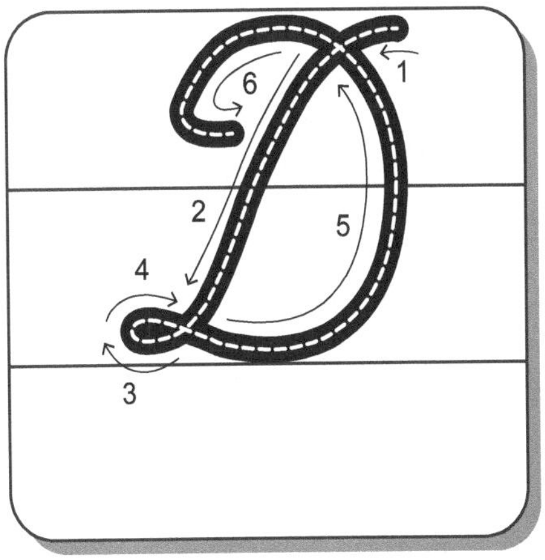

Dog

Date : ....

Teacher's Signature : ....

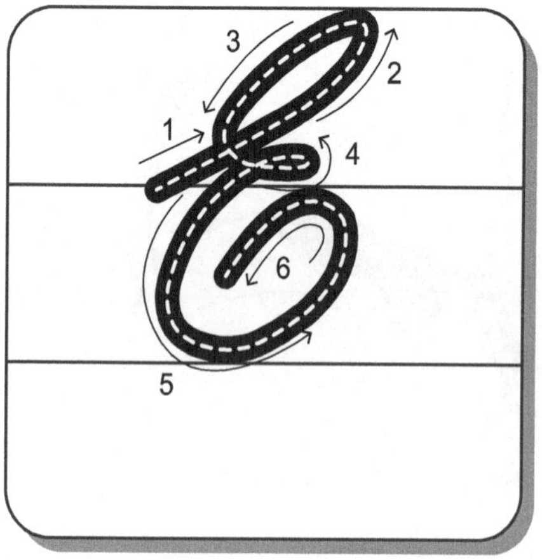

Egg

Date : ....

Teacher's Signature : ....

Fan

Date : ....

Teacher's Signature : ....

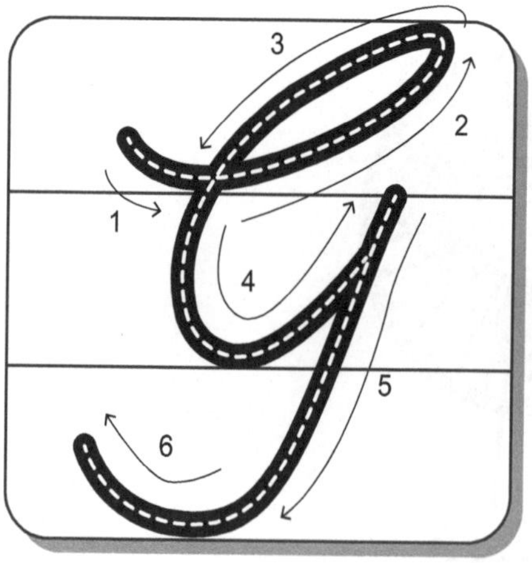

Grapes

Date : ....

Teacher's Signature : ....

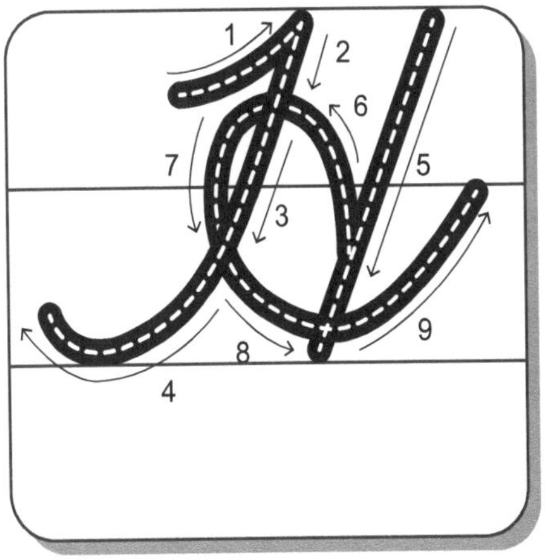

House

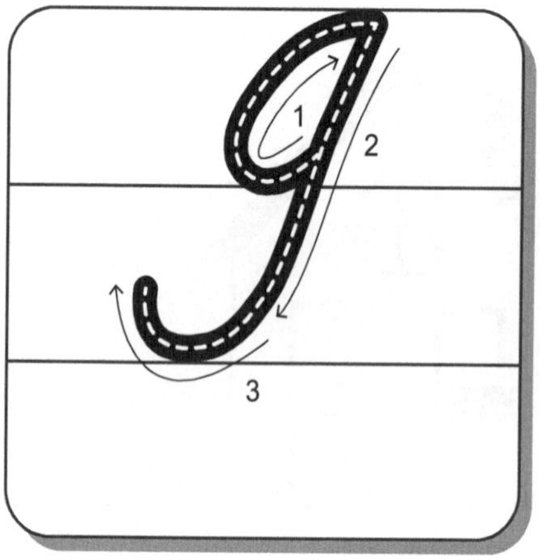

Ice-cream

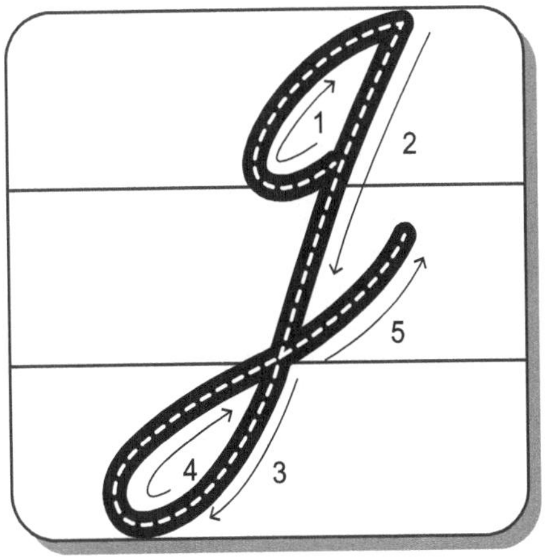

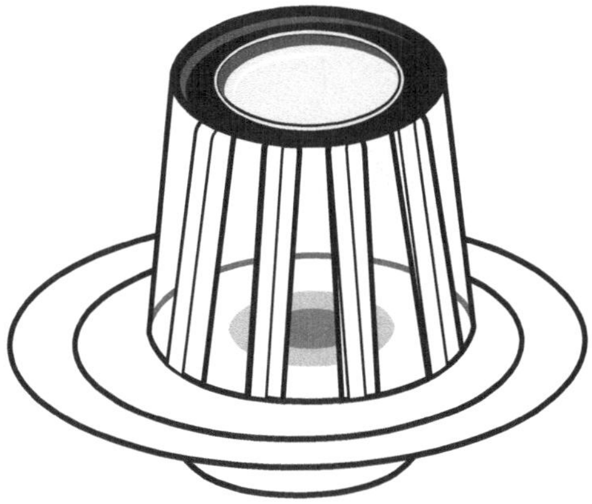

Jelly

Date : ....

Teacher's Signature : ....

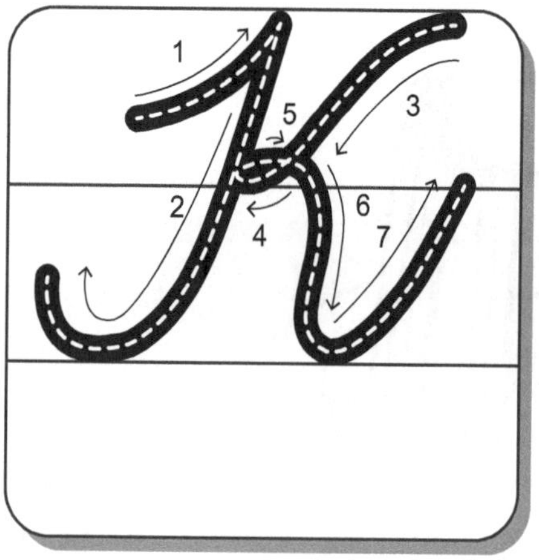

Key

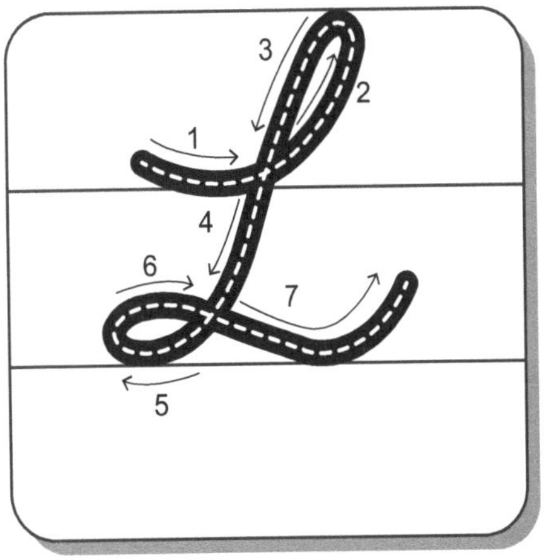

Lion

Date : ....

Teacher's Signature : ....

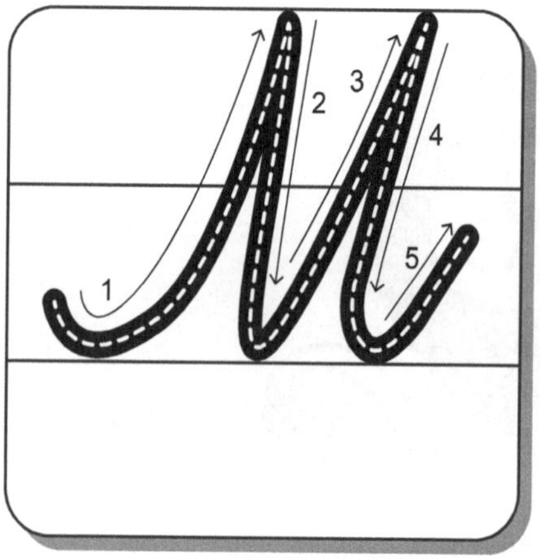

Moon

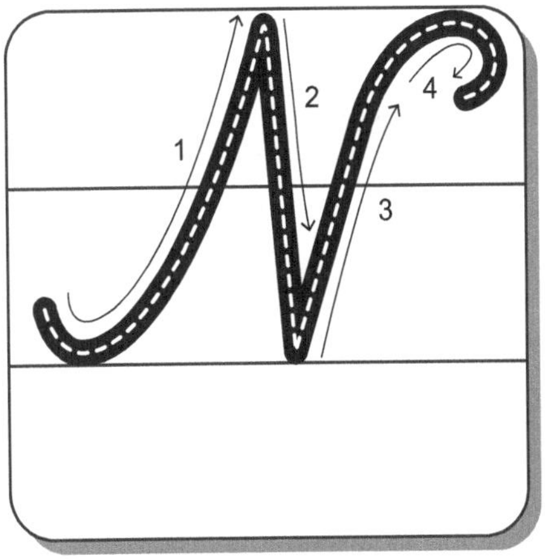

9

Nine

Date : ....

Teacher's Signature : ....

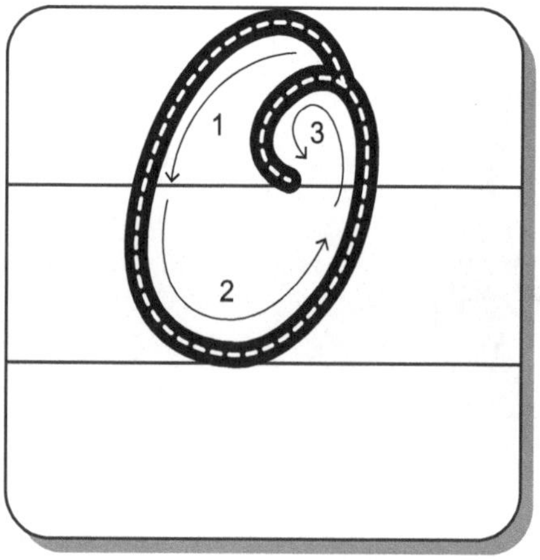

Onion

Pineapple

Date : ....

Teacher's Signature : ....

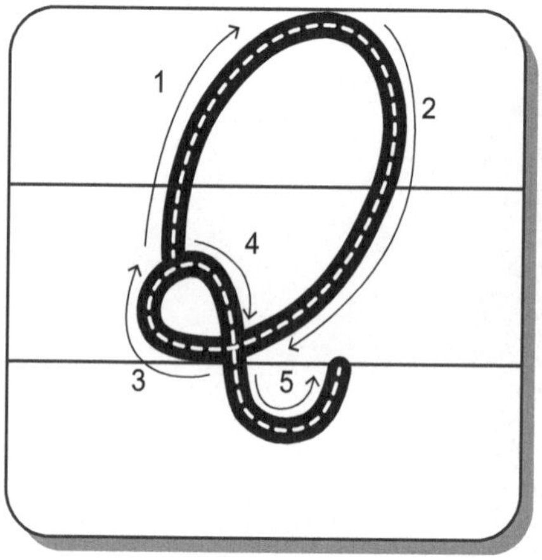

Queen

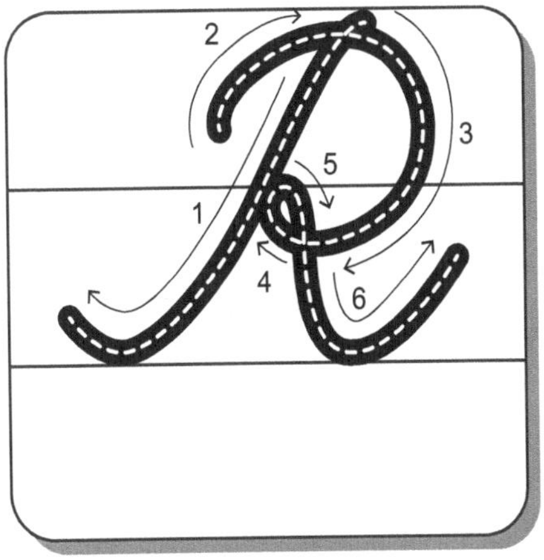

Rabbit

Date : ....

Teacher's Signature : ....

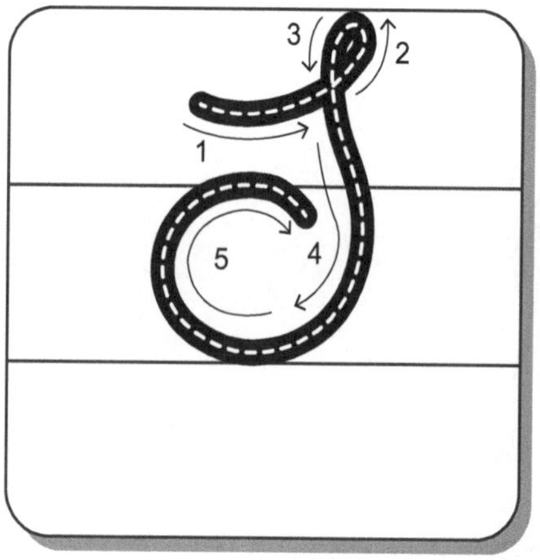

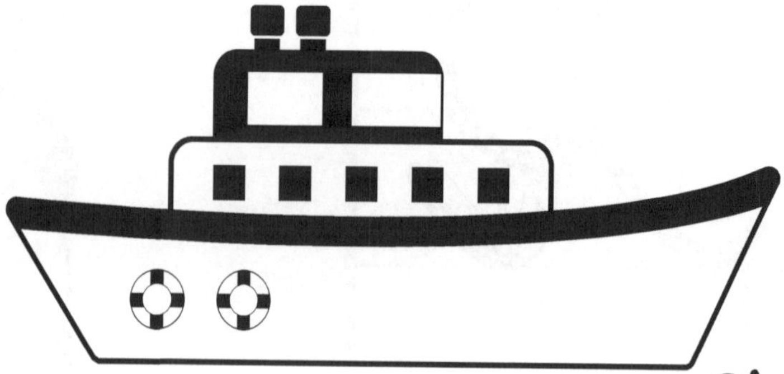

Ship

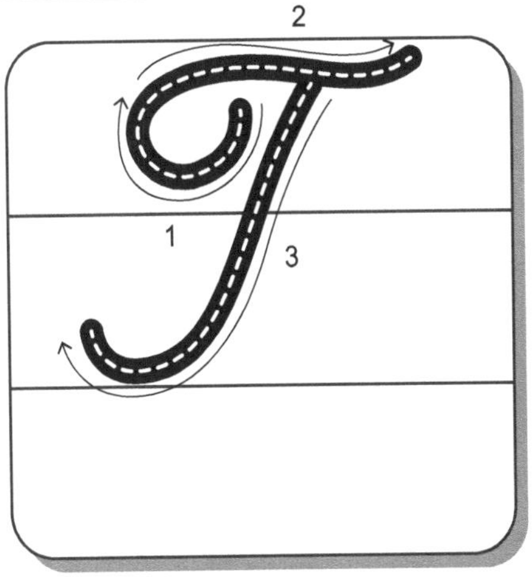

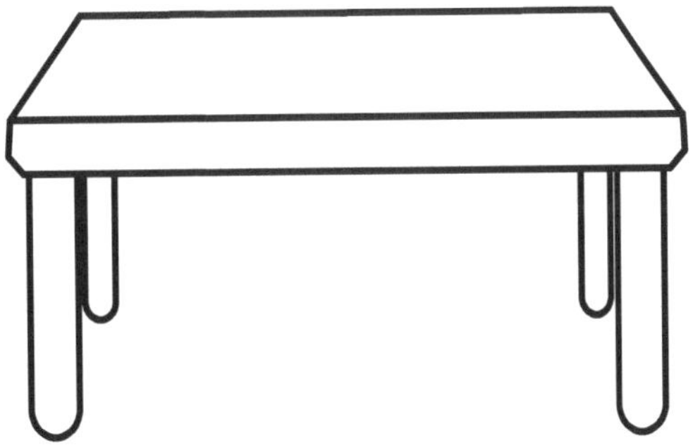

Table

Date : ....

Teacher's Signature : ....

Unicorn

Date : ....

Teacher's Signature : ....

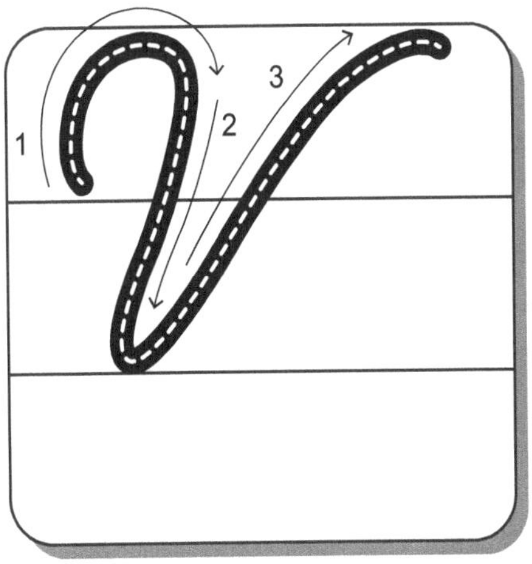

Van

Date : ....

Teacher's Signature : ....

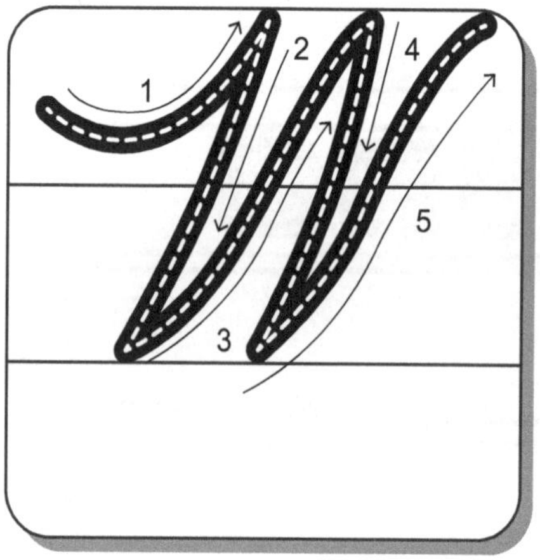

Window

Date : ....

Teacher's Signature : ....

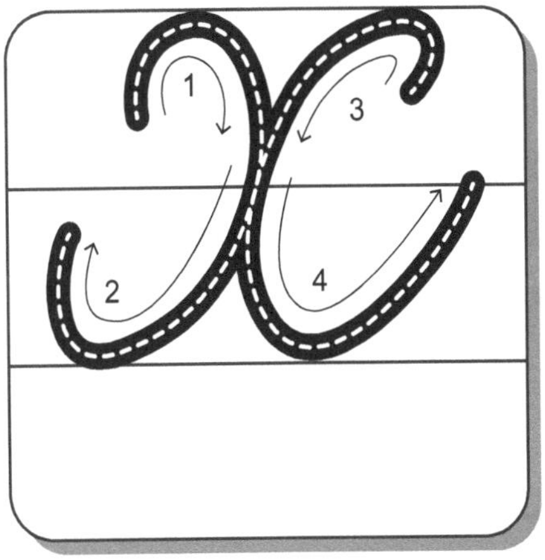

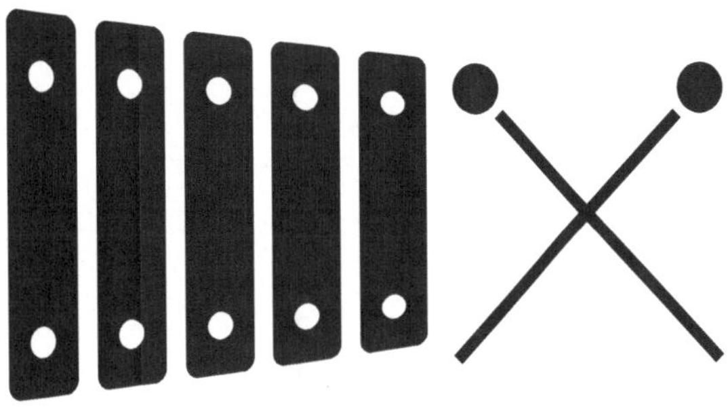

Xylophone

Date : ....

Teacher's Signature : ....

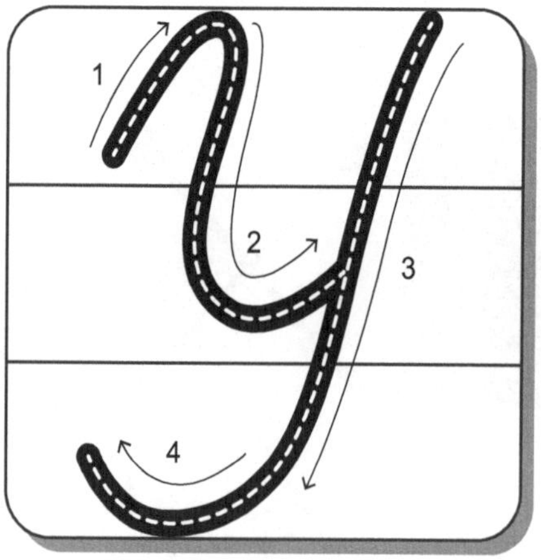

yo-yo

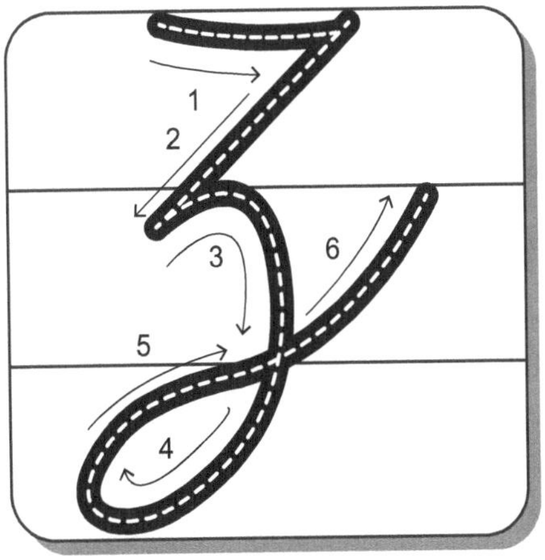

Zoo

Date : ....

Teacher's Signature : ....

Say and trace the letters.

A	B	C	D	E	F
G	H	I	J	K	L
M	N	O	P	Q	R
S	T	U	V	W	X
Y	Z				

Write the letters A to Z.

Write the missing letters from A to Z.

A		C		E	F
G			J		L
M		O			R
	T	U		W	
Y					

Write the letter that comes after the given letter.

U		X		L	
G		Q		R	

Write the letter that comes before the given letter.

	M		F		T
	J		G		O

Match and write the letters with objects they start with.

R

B

W

O

G

Y

M

E

Date : ....

Teacher's Signature : ....